The
Beachcomber's
Companion

The Beachcomber's Companion

An Illustrated Guide to Collecting and Identifying Beach Treasures

Anna Marlis Burgard

Illustrations by Jillian Ditner

CHRONICLE BOOKS

SAN FRANCISCO

Library of Congress Cataloging-in-Publication Data:

Names: Burgard, Anna Marlis, author.
Title: The beachcomber's companion / Anna Marlis
Burgard ; illustrations by Jillian Ditner.
Description: San Francisco : Chronicle Books, 2018.
Identifiers: LCCN 2017019840 | ISBN 9781452161167
(hardback)
Subjects: LCSH: Beachcombing. | Shells—Pictorial works. |
   Shells—Identification. | Shells—Collectors and collecting.
| BISAC: NATURE / Seashells.
Classification: LCC G532 .B87 2018 | DDC 910.914/
6—dc23 LC record available at https://lccn.loc.
gov/2017019840

Manufactured in China.

Illustrations by Jillian Ditner
Design by Jennifer Tolo Pierce
Cover title treatment by Pamela Johnson

10 9 8 7 6 5 4 3 2 1

Chronicle Books LLC
680 Second Street
San Francisco, California 94107
www.chroniclebooks.com

For Aunt Jo, whose gift of a bookbinding kit set me on my path.

Contents

Portrait of a Beachcomber   *8*

PART ONE: Identifications   *15*

Bivalves   *16*

Angel Wing   *18*

Coquina   *21*

Jingle   *22*

Oyster   *25*

Pen Shell   *26*

Northern Quahog   *28*

Razor   *31*

Scallop   *34*

Belles of the Bivalves   *37*

Gastropods   *40*

Auger   *42*

Baby's Ear   *45*

Common Nutmeg   *46*

Conch   *49*

Cone   *52*

Cowrie   *55*

Junonia   *57*

Keyhole Limpet   *61*

Moon Shell   *62*

Scotch Bonnet   *65*

Wentletrap   *66*

Whelk   *69*

More Gorgeous Gastropods   *70*

Echinoderms, Crustaceans, and Other Beach Treasures 72

Sand Dollar 74

Sea Star 77

A Cast of Crabs 80

Barnacle 83

Sea Urchin 86

Horseshoe Crab 89

Skate Egg Case 90

Sea Bean 92

Shark Tooth 97

Arrowhead 98

Sea Glass 101

Clay Baby 104

Toys, Shoes, and Other Flotsam 106

Message in a Bottle 109

PART TWO: A Beachcomber's Tool Kit 111

The Beachcomber's Commandments 112

Cleaning Seashells 118

The Collector's Travel Kit 122

Acknowledgments 124

Index 126

Portrait of a Beachcomber

The treasures we find at the beach are all pieces of an ocean's story; the shoreline is the introduction where we meet some of its characters and are given clues to its far-reaching communities. Beachcombing is a simple pleasure; the scanning of the surf line, along with the sounds of the waves and wind, helps create a sort of hypnotic state, releasing whatever else might be on our minds. Ancient beach hunters used shells to make tools and ornamental objects some one hundred thousand years ago. Collecting, as we understand it now, existed during the time of the pharaohs, but began on a more widespread basis when the Dutch took to the seas in the seventeenth century. Shells, mainly from Indonesia, rare at that time in Europe, could be more costly than paintings by Vermeer. A true "conchylomania" set in, driving people to spend outrageous sums to acquire an exotic shell before their friend or competitor had a chance to. Through the Victorian period, curiosity cabinets were filled with praiseworthy specimens; in the last century, diving and trawling gave easier access to once-elusive shells.

Some of history's notable collectors were Emperor Hirohito, Peter the Great, and Fidel Castro. The Smithsonian's National Museum of Natural History holds the world's largest collection, with more than twenty million mollusk specimens. A less grand, but no less passionate, amateur display is found in the Kenneth E. Stoddard Shell Museum in Boothbay, Maine—built inside a covered bridge—which sprang from Stoddard's World War II off-duty shell collecting in the South Pacific. Others have created grottoes on their properties with shells (including the famous subterranean chamber in Margate, England), or lined cottage walls with them. Most of us display our shells in much less formal ways—in old mason jars and baskets and shadow boxes, or on top of books or along window-sills, but we're no less proud of them, or less glad to be surrounded by the memories of finding them.

And of course, beachcombers' curiosities are piqued by more than the shells themselves—we're also hooked by the stories of the animals that make shells their homes and by our myriad finds' environments of origin. An arrowhead unearthed by the Chesapeake's waters on Smith Island, Maryland, connects its finder to a native hunter from the age of mastodons, who shaped it from jasper with a deer's antler. A European sea bean collector knows a drift seed traveled thousands of miles on the Atlantic's currents from a Costa Rican forest filled with the sounds of scarlet macaws and spider monkeys. A gleaming piece of frosted glass in Seaham, England, began its life as a bottle created by a Victorian factory worker.

Finding a bottle on Turks and Caicos with a message sealed decades before leads to the understanding of a stranger's struggle, or perhaps love. And happening upon a coveted junonia shell on Florida's Sanibel Island brings the collector into the life story of a deep-sea creature; people who find them get their photos in the local newspaper.

Beachcombers are excited about true albino shells, about dollhouse-scaled "littles," and chuckle about so-called "wedding shells"—varieties that aren't from surrounding seas but are brought in for nuptial celebrations, leading unaware visitors to believe they've found a rare shell, half a world away from the waters it called home. For many, the thrill of the hunt alone in a beautiful place is pleasure enough.

It isn't hard to spot us; we're the ones who are often more tanned on our backs than our fronts, given how much time we spend bent over looking at things (the "Sanibel stoop"), poking around in ropes of seaweed wrack and looking into tide pools. You'll see us coming off the beach just as others are starting their morning runs. We head out when everyone else is hunkering down through a tropical storm: we want to see what the churned-up waters will bring ashore, as the turbulence moves deeper shells up over reefs and sandbars and brings floating items from further afield. The lure of wide and deep washes of beautiful objects makes otherwise rational people take risks, including wading into still-ripping currents, with all manner of sharp, heavy shells knocking into our ankles and shins, and waves knocking us down, in what Shellinator Donnie Benton refers to as "PowerShelling."

We always know when the tide's going out, and we carry extra bags to pick up trash while we're moseying along. We're curious, compulsive, and can be a little covetous when someone finds our Holy Grail shell or sea bean or ocean-polished shard of glass. We also tend to be protectors of wildlife, and of their environment, and most of us will stop and tell people anything they want to know about the shell they just picked up (and give them one of ours as a swap if it means saving the live critter they've unwittingly found). Edward Perry, an avid sea bean collector, talks about the stages that beachcombers proceed through: there's the initial introduction to the sea's bounty, followed by studying to satisfy curiosity about the find, followed by hoarding of the treasures, and finally, sharing and swapping to complete a collection. At first, we can't believe our luck—there are so many shells; picking them up is an innocent pleasure. But pretty soon we cover all our surfaces with drying shells, and we start displaying them in various containers, and a sense of feeling filled up by the abundance of them all comes over us. It's alright when we visit the beach for a week or so, but if living by the sea, we can reach a tipping point. To make sure we're balancing our wish to build our collection with simply appreciating Mother Nature, we should consider repatriating our less perfect shells or donating them to schools. We should consider those who come behind us to search, and also the ecology of any given beach where that shell might be a hermit crab's next home or the bowl from which a shorebird sips rain.

My beachcombing roots run deep. When I was growing up, my family visited Atlantic islands every year, and as I grew older, I trekked to shores not only in the United States, but also in Europe and Africa. My love for all things ocean eventually led me to found the multimedia project *Islands of America: A River, Lake and Sea Odyssey*; I've now visited more than one hundred islands in North America, collecting salty little souvenirs along the way. Wherever I am, the community of beachcombers is there with me, treasure hunting, admiring the natural beauty, and feeling fortunate for whatever hours, days, or weeks we have to take it all in.

More than forty shells and other beach beauties are featured in these pages, offering both likely finds and more rare discoveries. If you'd like to learn about other elements of beachcombing, including driftwood, palm trees, sand, shelling clubs, and more, visit www.islandsofamerica.com and look for "The Beachcomber's Companion."

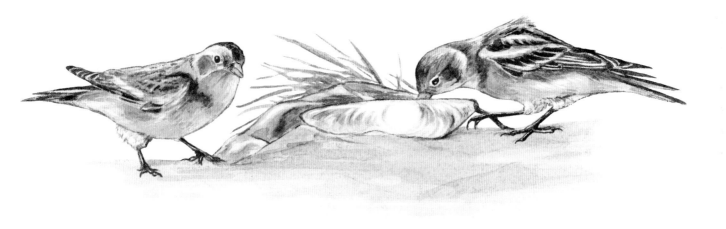

PART ONE

Identifications

Bivalves

Clams, mussels, oysters, and scallops are all *bivalves*—what we call their "shell" is one of the two valves that protect the creature. While most gastropods have *opercula* on their "feet" that are retracted like trapdoors to seal the snail inside, in most species of bivalves, adductor muscles pull the two hinged valves around them and seal tightly with interlocking grooves or "teeth," keeping the halves tightly aligned.

There are more than ten thousand species of bivalves in the world's waters. Generally, they're gilled filter feeders that contribute to the health of the environments they live in, because as they inhale and strain nutrients, they're also cleaning up toxins in the water—some larger varieties at the rate of a gallon per hour. While they don't have brains, they do have hearts, kidneys, stomachs, and intestinal tracts. Some, including scallops, have a form of eye along the edges of their *mantles* (the muscular layer that surrounds all mollusks' bodies) that allows them to sense light variations.

One of the remarkable differences among these creatures is their mobility: scallops "swim" by opening their valves, taking in water, and then squirting it back out, which propels them several feet ahead. Clams burrow into the sand or mud. Oysters and mussels affix themselves in communities to rocks, coral, and other surfaces, including mangrove roots and sunken ships. Their life spans also vary, from the shorter-lived coquina clam that lives less than a year to some varieties of quahog clam that can live more than one hundred years.

Most bivalves are capable of forming pearls, which are nothing more than layers of nacre—the smooth, iridescent layer often found on the inside of shells—produced around a small foreign object (for example, a grain of sand or a parasite) that's irritating the creature. The humble quahog clam makes purple pearls that might surprise you in your bowl of chowder. Sea scallop pearls, which have an unusual reflective quality, can be found in colors ranging from pink to orange to maroon. The majority of gem-quality pearls come from oysters, and most of these are now cultured, not natural, pearls.

Given the fragile nature of their joinery, it's always a special moment when you find a pair of shells intact. But even when you find just half of the whole, the variety and beauty of these bivalve houses make our sandy treasure hunting worthwhile.

* *Please note that some of the illustrations in this book are not to scale.*

ANGEL WING

There are few more graceful beings than the aptly named angel wing. Both beautiful and tough, they're the steel magnolias of the sea. Housed in a delicate and sculpted shell similar to fine bisque porcelain, this clam can burrow 2 feet [61 cm] down into tidal sand and clay (and even soft rocks like shale) without damaging itself, by using its muscles and raised ridges to grip and twist along. While it's rare to happen upon the two halves still hinged together (unlike most clams, they have weak muscles and can't fully close their shells, so damage is more common), a single "wing" is a fairly common find. They can be quite large, up to 7 inches [17 cm] or so, and are pure white.

Angel wings, also known as piddocks, are one of the meatier clams, making them a popular choice for seafood recipes. In Cuba and Puerto Rico, they're considered a delicacy when roasted with herbs and cheeses. On France's Normandy coast, they're pickled in vinegar. The clams grow so quickly—reaching a marketable size in just six months—that they're being considered for aquaculture farming in Florida.

One species of European angel wing has a superpower: it can glow in the dark. Back in the first century, Pliny the Elder wrote, "It is the nature of these fish to shine in darkness . . . to glitter both in the mouth of persons masticating them and in their hands, and even on the floor and on their clothes when drops fall from them, making it clear beyond all doubt that their juice possesses a property that we should marvel at."

While as living creatures angel wings are strong enough to bore into rock, their shells can be brittle once they come ashore and so must be packed especially carefully for the trip home (see page 122 for tips).

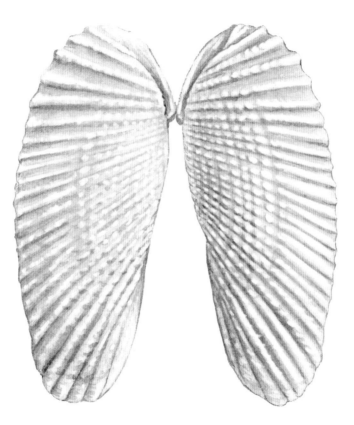

COQUINA

If any bivalve could be "happy as a clam," it would be the cheerfully colored coquina. These tiny clams flip themselves upright when the waves pull back out to sea, quickly burrowing down into the swash zone (the stirred-up layer of water that surges up onto the sand after a wave breaks) like a synchronized team. The coquina, also known as a digger boy, bean, or wedge clam, is the butterfly of the beach—with a life span of only four months to a year or so, where other clams can live a hundred years or more. When they've given up their ghosts and leave behind their shells, they look like a rainbow of wings on the sand. As abandoned shells are compressed over the ages beneath the weight of the sea, they're transformed into a light, porous rock. The Spanish used the coquina rock to build St. Augustine, Florida's fort Castillo de Marcos in 1695; the material was able to absorb the impact of cannonballs without shattering.

Coquinas are a favorite snack for shorebirds and other beach creatures. They're edible for people, too; in some locales they're cooked in a brothy soup. You need, however, to be fairly patient to dine on them—first parking them in water so they can purge the sand from their system before you eat the ¼ inch [6 mm] or so Lilliputian morsels.

The shells are now used to make pussywillow buds in flower-shaped arrangements. In the nineteenth century, they helped to form elaborate sailors' valentines—shell designs in hexagonal glass-topped boxes that became famous as souvenirs for those at sea to give their loved ones. Whether you have a knack for such craft forms or not, these delicate shells are welcome additions to any collection.

JINGLE

My first prize shell was a jingle I found on the beach in Ocean City, Maryland. It was bigger and sturdier than most you see, about the size of an old fifty-cent piece, and a deep orange. I displayed it proudly in my bedroom, leading my parents' dinner guests upstairs to admire it. Decades later, I'm still drawn to their translucent shine like a magpie. You can hear the tinkling that gives the shell its name when the surf tosses them on shore, or when the wind catches them in chimes on coastal porches.

Jingles are known colloquially as mermaid's money, mermaid scales, and sea witch fingernails.

They're found in shades of white, yellow, orange, gray, and even black. You usually see their rounded top halves, because their flatter bottom shells attach to rocks and other surfaces (categorizing them as *epifaunal*). Unlike most bivalves, their bottom shells also mold to the surface they attach to. When you do find the bottoms, you'll see a hole that serves as their anchoring point for their *byssus*— the patch of filaments that bivalves use (sometimes called a "beard") to hold them fast against crashing waves.

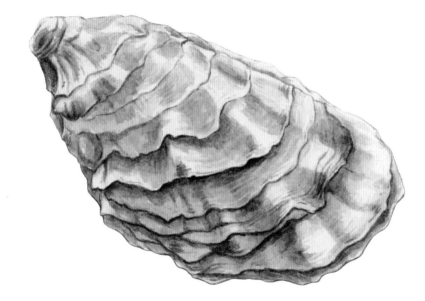

OYSTER

Rough and stained, the Atlantic oyster (called Chincoteague "salts" in my ancestors' Tidewater region) isn't a handsome shell, although it's sometimes used as a decorative element on lighting fixtures, crushed to make oyster shell driveways, or encased in a kind of lime–oyster shell stucco called "tabby" that can be seen on Southern homes. The Atlantic's cousins, including the imported Kumamoto and the tiny Olympia of the Pacific Northwest, don't boast elegant shells, either, but anyone who's been to an oyster bar knows oysters come in a nice variety of sizes and shapes, cups and fluting, so they can still add a lot of interest to a collection.

Lots of people along North America's coasts make their livelihood from these critters; to honor this industry, both Mississippi and Virginia named the Atlantic oyster their state shell. In Southern spots like Edisto Island, South Carolina, oyster roasts are a part of life; they're harvested from resident oyster beds and steamed over open fires. People bring shucking knives in leather sheaths and look for the lucky little pea crabs tucked inside the shells. They grow up knowing how to open oysters much like Marylanders are raised to know how to pick a crab, or people in Maine learn how to crack into a lobster at a young age. Oyster shells, humble as they are, bring good times to mind.

PEN SHELL

Silkworms and spiders aren't the only creatures known for producing interesting fibers. Pen shell clams, called "sea sheep" by the ancient Chinese, have a gland that manufactures a filament collectively called a byssus that was once used to make luxurious textiles. This "mermaid silk" even made an appearance in Jules Verne's *Twenty Thousand Leagues Under the Sea*, with the *Nautilus*'s crew wearing "fan-mussel fabric." Today there's a woman on the Sardinian island of Sant'Antioco who dives for the noble pen clam that makes this rarified fiber. She collects the byssus, dries and combs it, and then weaves it into small patches of golden cloth.

The byssus serves as an anchor for the pen on the sea floor where it buries itself. When storms uproot the clams, they're tossed onto shore. On Sanibel Island, Florida, pens wash up in such quantities that people make elaborate sculptures with them; they use the shells to outline clover and heart shapes that are yards wide and then fill the shapes with a host of smaller shells. Some furniture designers use the shells to form pieced veneers for tables. The pen shells' triangular forms themselves, while distinct, aren't usually prized by collectors; they're brown, and some have tubular spines that make them look a little like a ginger grater (and also make them painful to step on). One of the largest bivalves around, some varieties can reach 1 foot [30.5 cm] or more in length.

Pen clams are edible. Used like a firm scallop, they're called *tairagi* by sushi chefs. They're also a staple food for sea stars and horse conchs, among other marine predators.

NORTHERN QUAHOG

The northern quahog is at first glance a humble shell. Living its life in the mud, it's thick and inelegant, but it hides beauty away on the inside. It's in steady supply on North American Atlantic beaches, either whole or in its many purple and white shards. These heavy shells are more likely to be picked up for use as sand castle–building tools or ashtrays than for ooh-and-ah collection additions. I hadn't paid any real attention to them until I visited Stony Creek Gifts at the Gay Head lighthouse in Aquinnah, on Martha's Vineyard. In a display case were gorgeous pieces of jewelry made from shells by Berta Welch, a member of the Wampanoag tribe. These are not of "resort shop" quality but are rather small works of intricate craftsmanship made from quahogs, with mother-of-pearl accents.

The designs are interpretations of Wampanoag *wampum*—shell beads made into belts and other objects, to be worn, given as gifts, or used as proof of authority like a license might be today; the uses were many, of sacred, diplomatic, and everyday natures. The weaving of wampum belts is a sort of writing by means of colored beads, in which the various designs denote different ideas according to an accepted system—a kind of universal language, irrespective of spoken languages. The Wampanoags have lived on the Vineyard for thousands of years, so the reinvention of this craft has deep significance. And to this day, wampum is used in Onondaga Nation ceremonies to honor a new chief.

{continued}

In 2006, a 507-year-old ocean quahog (a relative of the northern) was found buried hundreds of feet down off of Iceland's northern coast by a team from Bangor University. The shell was nicknamed "Ming," for the Chinese dynasty in power when it was born (in England, Henry VIII was not yet king).

Once you know all this, it's hard to look at the quahog the same way again: its simple exterior masks noble leanings. As a filter-feeding marine animal, one clam can clean a gallon of water in an hour, so they're steward mollusks, cleaning up the waters as oysters do. They're also pretty tasty, presented as littleneck and cherrystone clams in chowders or on the half shell.

RAZOR

Razor clams give themselves away in the sand with keyhole-shaped cavities or "dimples" above the tunnels they carve out while burrowing; they'll also announce themselves by squirting water back up the hole if disturbed by people walking above them. They also might peek their bodies out above the sand, in a motion called "necking," when the waves recede. Some beachcombers feel their shells before they see them, as stepping on their thin, sharp edges can be painful!

Razors are expert diggers, opening and closing their shells with enough force to set in motion a process called *thixotropy* whereby their actions thin the liquids in the surrounding sand, allowing the razors to quickly burrow down as far as one-third of a mile [536 m]. This skill has caught the attention of mechanical engineers at Massachusetts Institute of Technology and other institutions, who are interested in mimicking this process for potential marine robotics projects.

All razor clams have what look like the annual rings of a tree trunk on their shells, but while it's true that mollusks continue to add to their shells' size (or thickness, in some cases) as they grow throughout their lives, the stripes on razor and other clams are not true age indicators. It's only by sawing into a shell and looking at its cross section that a real understanding of its age and growth cycles can be reached.

{continued}

Also known as spoot ("spout" in a Scottish dialect), stickbait, and finger oysters in other parts of the world, razor clams are cousins to the thinner jackknife clam also found on U.S. shores. Fishermen often use the meat as bait, and many coastal communities, tribal and otherwise, cook them up; their flavor has been likened to something between scallops and squid.

On the beach at night alone,
As the old mother sways her to and fro singing her husky song,
As I watch the bright stars shining, I think a thought of the clef
of the universes and of the future. — WALT WHITMAN

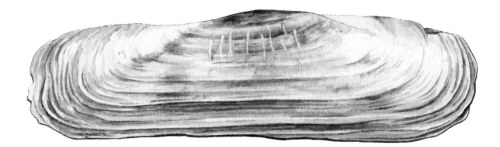

SCALLOP

The scallop shell is an iconic form—a shorthand image representing all things nautical, like an anchor. Its familiar fan shape has been incorporated into architectural and artistic works for millennia. Sandro Botticelli famously presented a woman surfing to shore on a scallop shell in *The Birth of Venus*. The shell was said to have been carried by Saint James on his travels to Spain from the Middle East; it's said he would ask strangers for no more water and food than would fit in its bowl, to prevent burdening those who could spare little. Pilgrims traveling the routes to Catedral de Santiago de Compostela in Spain (where St. James is believed to be interred), Canterbury Cathedral in England, and Mont-St-Michel in France used the scallop as their symbol. It eventually became the image for pilgrimage itself, and still today some pilgrims to Catedral de Santiago attach a scallop shell to their backpacks.

The Wampanoag tribe has harvested scallops from Martha's Vineyard's Menemsha Pond for untold generations; today, heaping *middens* (shell mounds) dot their tribal lands in Aquinnah, and strings of lights made with the shells illuminate their porches on summer evenings. At the other end of the Atlantic Seaboard, prior to the Spanish colonial era, Florida's Calusa people (the "Shell Indians") used scallop shells as plates, cups, hide scrapers, and weights for their woven-palm fishing nets.

{continued}

There are nearly three hundred species of bay and sea scallops, living from polar regions to the tropics, which is good news for shell collectors. This group of clams offers a rich and colorful array of patterns and colors, from calicos to stripes to solid neon-hued varieties, adding to their popularity.

Unlike its bivalve cousins, including the mussel and oyster, a scallop can't shut its shell up tight, which keeps it at some risk. On the other hand, its mantle sports anywhere from ten to one hundred blue eyes, which let it know when danger's afoot by allowing it to sense dark, light, and movement. Scallops are set even further apart from bivalve cousins by their distinct advantage of being able to swim by means of jet propulsion with the intake and expulsion of water, courtesy of their adductor muscles—the bit we eat. They stymie their predators—typically sea stars, crabs, rays, and snails—with this "clapping" motion of their shells; because of this behavior, they've earned the moniker "the butterflies of the sea." While other escape behaviors exist among bivalves—including the razor clam's rapid burrowing technique and the cockle's use of a muscular foot to launch away from predators—scallops would rule the bivalve Olympics.

BELLES OF THE BIVALVES

A number of the most sought-after bivalve shells belong to the Veneridae family, which is better known by the common name Venus clams. In his *Systema Naturae*, the eighteenth-century Swedish naturalist Carl Linnaeus identified one of these shells in what one of his peers called a "licentious" fashion, likening the area where the two valves join to parts of a woman's anatomy. His fellow academic thought scientific accounts should be "chaste and delicate"; a century later, the *Encyclopedia Britannica* called the descriptions "obscene allusions." Given how he responded to the shells, it's no surprise that the Swede named them for the goddess of love.

The "ovoid" (oval) sunray Venus sports a lavender, gray, and taupe plaid that if baked in the sun (or steamed for dinner) turns more coral pink. It's a sturdy clam that Floridian aquaculturists think could be the next marine farming boom, given their plump, sweet, and pale flesh paired with their pretty shells.

The "trigonal" (triangular) imperial Venus—sometimes called the Pawley's Island shell because of its prevalence there, as well as a marketing campaign by a local jeweler—is small at 1.5 inches [4 cm] or so. But it has a big fan club because of its "beveled escutcheons" or fluted concentric ribs, and the range of colors it can be found in.

{continued}

imperial Venus

sunray Venus

Wedding Cake Venus

But the grande dame must be the Wedding Cake Venus, found on coasts in the Tasmanian Sea. Mainly creamy white, but sometimes tinged with pink, its frilly ribs look like frosted tiers. It is a sculptural work of art.

Beautiful but brainless, these creatures manage to be amazingly sculpted and exotically painted. While we know that genetic coding and neural impulses are behind their patterns and fluting, even the experts don't fully understand *why* the shells are so highly designed, or how they create their pigments.

Gather a shell from the strewn beach,

And listen at its lips: they sigh

The same desire and mystery,

The echo of the whole sea's speech.

— DANTE GABRIEL ROSSETTI

Gastropods

When you think of the myriad mollusk houses that tumble to shore, you realize that the world's coastlines are jeweled beyond measure. And yet what we see as we scan the surf line is only a hint of the world beneath the waves, of how these snails and clams and other creatures live and interact—and of the lives their shells take on after they're lifted from the sand.

The diversity that the Gastropoda class of mollusks represents is a perfect example of this bounty; their numbers are second only to insects, with estimates ranging from fifty to more than one hundred thousand species. Gastropods are snails that are generally housed in spiraled shells of a stunning variety of shapes and sizes; they build on their shells' outer edge as they grow, remaining in them for life. Moon snails are round and fit in your hand; horse conchs can reach 2 feet [61 cm] in length and have spires on their shells that look like a turret (and they're fierce hunters, smothering their prey); augers' shells are triangular and skinny; baby's ears look almost like jellyfish that wear a small, flat shell hat; and sundials are shaped like a labyrinth.

Some snails can hop by extending their muscular feet. They live in both cold and warm waters and can even be found in the deepest, darkest reaches of the sea around thermal vents, where one Indian Ocean species, the scaly-foot snail, is sheathed in iron-enriched armor. Marine snail shells might be striped like the lightning whelks', "lettered" like some olives, or spotted like junonias. They might have rough, spiky surfaces like the murex or smooth, glossy ones like the cowrie. Their shell features include knobs and whorls and ribs.

The shells these fascinating creatures leave behind have served in military, religious, and cultural ceremonies for thousands of years. Conch and triton bugles, like those still seen at sundowner ceremonies in Hawaii, hold importance throughout Pacific and Indian Ocean cultures. On Okinawa, Japan, Ryukyuan priestesses "fed" rice into conch shells that represented their mirror spiritual selves. In Buddhist mythologies, the conch shells belonging to heroes were named and had the power to dispel evil spirits.

While we pick these shells up because they're beautiful, there's always much more to know about both the animal and the many ways we humans have found to use their shells.

AUGER

The narrow triangles known as auger shells are easy to spot. With their pointed, spiraled design, they look like miniature unicorn horns or narwhal tusks, but they're named for their resemblance to auger drill bits. This group of shells, which includes about three hundred varieties, inspired some colorful names, including hectic auger and inconstant auger. The flame auger from Guantánamo Bay, Cuba, pictured here, is a larger species at about 4 inches [10 cm] in length, with slightly rounded upper whorls. The whorls of the common Atlantic auger (found from Virginia down to the West Indies) are flatter and have the ribbing that most varieties sport.

Auger shells can be found around the globe in warmer waters, often in the intertidal zone between low and high tide. Like their relative the cones, many augers pierce their prey with a toothy barb that injects a paralytic toxin. What's bad news for marine worms may be good news for humans, as the toxin is being studied for use as a painkiller.

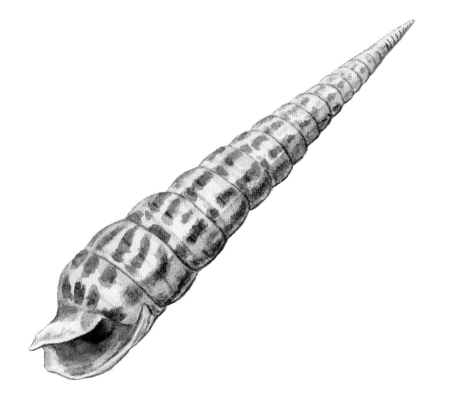

BABY'S EAR

The baby's ear wins the award for "Shell Least Likely to Be Associated with Its Creator." The shell is a graceful slip of a thing, like a 1- to 2-inch [2.5- to 5-cm] abalone: flat, oval, and slightly corded or ribbed. The snail, however, is an ungainly blob, with looks akin to a jellyfish wearing a tiny shell beret. The snail, like a few other gastropods including its relative the moon snail, almost completely surrounds its shell at times—it's an inside-out sort of critter.

The shell can be pure white, or, after extended stays in sediment, colored to a wide range of marbled hues from pale yellow to blue gray to slate black. The shells are so lightweight that they float up high and are deposited above the *wrack lines* (the tangled strands of seaweed, reeds, and other bits you see on shore), but they're strong enough to withstand the surf—you'll rarely find broken ones. The common baby's ear can be found from Maryland down to Brazil; maculated baby's ears, which sport spots, can be found in North and South Carolina and sometimes over on Florida's western shores.

Baby's ears should probably also win the "Cutest Shell Award"—there's something dear about them, and something soothing, too, when rubbed between your fingers like a seaborne prayer bead.

COMMON NUTMEG

The common nutmeg's surface is technically referred to as "latticed" or "beaded," but it looks as though its maker thinly rolled out some dough, pressed window screening into it, then rolled it up into a fanciful dinner roll shape. It's found from the shores of North Carolina down through Brazil.

There are more than two hundred varieties of nutmegs, with coloring ranging from banded grays and browns, or, with this "common" type, cream with orange-brown patches. There's an obese nutmeg that pushes out on its whorls as if trying to fit into clothes of yesteryear (otherwise referred to as *orbicular* and *globose*—rounded to the point of being almost spherical) as well as a

Clark's slim nutmeg. One variety found on Costa Rican beaches, the Miller's nutmeg shell, looks like it's unraveling, with its whorls dramatically pulled apart (or *unsutured*)—they look as though they're in motion.

There's the blood-mouthed nutmeg in Galapagos waters with an orange-red *aperture ring* (kind of like a door frame to the shell's house); it may have sanguine accents, but the Cooper's nutmeg found from Monterey, California, down to Baja California in Mexico is an aquatic vampire that would be better suited to that coloring, as it attaches itself to angel sharks and Pacific electric rays, making small cuts in their skin until it taps a

{continued}

vein with its siphon, then feasts on their blood. The ray doesn't flinch, and the snail seems unaffected by the ray's one-kilowatt electric charge. While a little macabre, Cooper's do leave behind very pretty shells, with blue-gray and apricot banding and darker mahogany stripes.

It is perhaps a more fortunate destiny to have a taste for collecting shells than to be born a millionaire. — ROBERT LOUIS STEVENSON

CONCH

There are few more memorable moments in film than when Ursula Andress emerged from the sea in *Dr. No* with a prize queen conch shell in her hand. This majestic, knobby, pink-lipped snail can live for thirty years or more if left undisturbed; it forms its distinctive frilled edge at about three years old. Prior to that, the juvenile animals and their shells are referred to as "rollers" because they're tossed about in the waves more easily thanks to their light weight and symmetry. James Bond's creator, Ian Fleming, lived in Jamaica, where the film was set; his significant shell collection was in his residence.

The queen conch has a rich history of symbolism. When Key West, Florida, threatened to secede in 1982, the region's citizens chose the queen conch as the flag's emblem in honor of their moniker "The Conch Republic"; to this day, the community hosts an annual conch shell–blowing contest. On the Caribbean island Dominica, fishmongers sound conch horns to announce their wares, and in the West Indies, they're blown during cricket matches. This follows ancient traditions in India, Japan, and Hawaii of conch (and triton) trumpets being used for religious and ceremonial purposes, dating back many thousands of years. It's said the "om" chant that's so integral to meditation is based on the sound from a conch shell, and that the sound gave protection from dangerous animals, wayward spirits, and enemy troops.

{continued}

Like the junonia and the scotch bonnet, the queen conch is a sought-after shell. Because it was overfished for its meat for decades, it was added to the Convention for the International Trade of Endangered Species in 1992, which means that tourists can have them confiscated from their luggage. Pay attention, as ever, to local laws. Florida allows possession as long as it's clear that the snail wasn't killed for its shell.

While the queen is spectacular, there are others of note. The palm-size Florida fighting conch, for instance, is a glossy, thick-shelled beauty that's found in a number of shades of brown, and sometimes, as a pure white albino. The turreted horse conch, Florida's state shell (pictured on page 120), can reach 2 feet (61 cm) in length; its animal is bright orange.

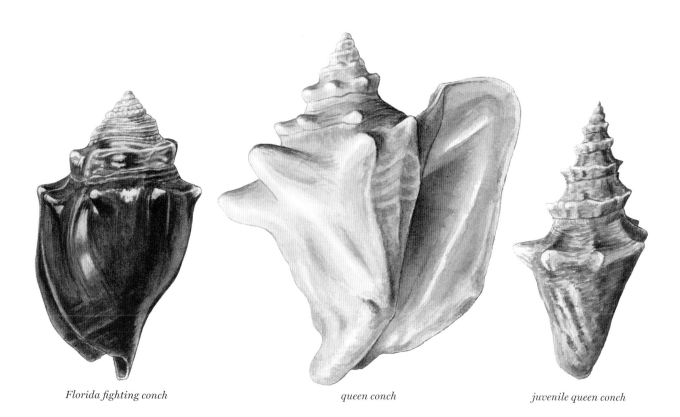

Florida fighting conch

queen conch

juvenile queen conch

CONE

Cone snails are found around the world and leave behind heavy, smooth, and beautifully patterned shells, like porcelain. Beads made from some varieties' flattened or *obconical* spires have been found at archeological sites dating back many thousands of years. Some cones, such as the Glory of the Seas, can fetch hundreds of dollars at auction.

But take care when reaching for a cone while snorkeling or diving, or even in tidal pools! The deadliest mollusk in the world is the Indo-Pacific geographic cone, nicknamed the "cigarette snail"

because once it jabs its poisoned harpoon into your flesh, you have about as much time as it takes to smoke a cigarette to say your good-byes. There's no antivenin to its powerful neurotoxin. All five-hundred-odd cone snail species have venom glands with *conotoxins* of varying intensities used to paralyze their prey. The good news is some of the proteins found in these toxins have been used in the development of the painkiller Ziconotide, said to be more effective than morphine without the addictive effects.

marbled cone

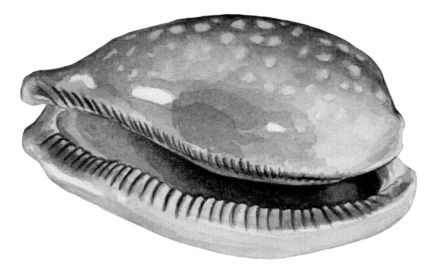

deer cowrie

COWRIE

Throughout history, cowries have been culturally important. Because of the two rows of "teeth" on their underside, they're sometimes referred to as the "mouth of God," which led to their presence in Yoruban divination and carried over into Santeria practices. They've been used as currency, and as fertility amulets in North America, Europe, Africa, and Asia. In Japan, women held a cowrie shell in their hand to ease deliveries, much as women in the Outer Hebrides used the Mary's sea bean (see page 95). In Indian Kerala astrological divination, 108 cowrie shells are used after being bathed in sacred waters; practitioners even speak of "protecting" their cowries.

Cowries are a family of more than two hundred species that come in a range of sizes, from wee Pacific dew-drop cowries that can measure only ¼ inch [6 mm] to the largest species, the Atlantic deer cowrie (named for its coloring and "fawn" spots), which measures up to 7 inches [17.5 cm] and is found on offshore banks of the southeast Atlantic, parts of the Gulf of Mexico, and Cuba. Unless you're a diver, you're unlikely to see them, and even then, these snails are mainly nocturnal, tucking themselves away in crevices during the day. It takes a good storm's heaving currents to roll these heavy shells from their hideaways and up over sandbars and onto the beach, so finding one is a stroke of luck.

{continued}

Sand-burrowing gastropods, like cowries, olives, and moon snails, wrap their mantles around their shells as if bracing for a winter wind. Some of these mantles are as spectacularly patterned as their shells. Those of cowries come in a truly remarkable array of fashionable stripes, dots, and abstract patterns in pinks, browns, and oranges. Some even have what's referred to as a "fringe," a frilly edge to their flesh.

When they do make it out of the ocean, cowrie shells are sometimes carved like helmet shell cameos for souvenirs, although generally of a rougher tourist level than fine gem quality. One of the rarest shells in the world, the white-toothed cowrie, can fetch a sizable amount at auction. From their glossy exteriors (formed in part by having a higher crystal density than most other snail shells) to their zipperlike opening, cowries are desirable additions to any collection.

JUNONIA

There's a "big five" animal checklist on African safaris that includes the elephant, cape buffalo, black rhinoceros, lion, and, the most elusive of all, the leopard. Seashell collecting reminds me of a safari sometimes, as we search for gems disguised by seaweed and surrounding shells, half buried in the sand. Serious beachcombers have certain shells that will prompt happy dances when found, and a "life list" that gets checked off over the decades as more and more are discovered.

If shelling had its own "big five," the junonia would definitely make the list. It's a mollusk akin to the leopard: exotic, hard to find, and a cause for celebration once you do. In Florida, local Sanibel Island newspapers feature fortunate finders; a street there is even named for it—it's a celebrity seashell. Those near you when you're lucky enough to "snag a J" might be a little "shellous." It's so sought after that finding only a shard is considered worthy of mention. The worst possible luck would be that after a lifetime of looking for one, it finally crosses your path—but the snail still inhabits it, rendering it unethical (and illegal) to take. It's kind of like having a family member win the lottery—odds are the opportunity will never come near you again.

Junonias are *volutes*, a family of predatory snail represented by nearly two hundred species;

{continued}

the name volute comes from *voluta* or "scroll" in Latin, a reference to their elegant whorls. Before shrimp trawlers brought junonias up in their nets or divers could search for them, collectors had to rely on the churned-up seas to toss them onto shore. In the height of Victorian collecting, there were only four physical examples in all of Europe. While more are found today (which is why you can buy them online—no sheller would surrender theirs), they remain the jewel in the crown of most American shell collections, and one variety, the Johnstone's junonia, is Alabama's state shell.

I seem to have been only like a boy playing on the seashore, and diverting myself in now and then finding a smoother pebble or a prettier shell than ordinary, whilst the great ocean of truth lay all undiscovered before me. — SIR ISAAC NEWTON

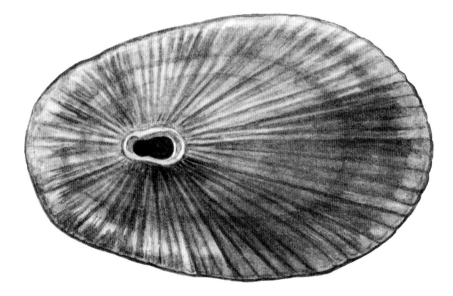

KEYHOLE LIMPET

Spruce Island is an emerald bit of terra firma in Alaska's remote Kodiak archipelago, a thirty-minute open skiff ride from Kodiak Island. St. Michael's Skete, a Serbian Orthodox outpost, is on Spruce. The skete's priests live simply; their diet consists mainly of foraged berries, mushrooms, and salmon, which are plentiful in the waters surrounding the island. Puffins fly overhead, and on the beach, you can find, among other shells, keyhole limpets. In the little time they have to spare after prayer and providing for their necessities, the priests make Christmas ornaments including a *baidarka* (an Aleutian kayak) design that incorporates keyhole limpet shells used for the rower's traditional Haida tribal hat. The Haida, an indigenous people of the Pacific Northwest Coast, used to string these shells together for rattles; one of their folktales includes a ghost shaking one as it walks through a town at night, prompting nightmares for all who hear it, like a Pacific Northwest Jacob Marley with his chains.

The interesting conical shape and texture of keyhole limpets' shells is called *reticulate*, or netlike; their "pitch" changes depending on how rough the waters are where they anchor onto rocks, as flatter shells can better resist heavier surf. Similar to baby's ear shells, this snail seems to wear its shell like a little cap over its exposed body rather than being protected by it. They can be found all over the world on beaches framing both cold and warm seas.

While the shells are lovely, one of the creatures they protect, the giant keyhole limpet snail of the Baja Peninsula, serves a higher purpose. A protein in its blood called *hemocyanin*, similar to hemo-globin in humans, is used in a drug (sold in other countries) as a treatment for bladder cancer and is being researched as relief for other medical conditions. Happily, the research is harmless to the snail—they aren't injured during the blood-extraction process.

MOON SHELL

The moon snail's shell is like a giant worry bead—the lovely shape is calming when rolled between your fingers. In banded shades of gray, black, and brown, it's also handsome. The creature itself is far less attractive than its housing; when it lets its mantle loose, it looks like a melted substance is oozing out.

It may be ugly, but it has skills. When you find a clam shell with a perfect hole in it, the moon snail is often to blame. It drills into its prey with an effective tooth-like appendage called a *radula* and pours a corrosive acid into the hole until it pushes through. The snail then drips an enzyme into the shell to make its dining easier: since it doesn't have the gripping abilities of a sea star or the cracking abilities of a crab, it has to liquefy its clam meal to slurp it out of the otherwise intact shell. There are no moon snail straws, but somehow it gets the job done.

Also known as a shark's eye, there are about three hundred species of moon snails. One of the most interesting facts about them is how they lay eggs. When you find what looks like a plastic letter "C" on the sand, a smooth, flat object with sometimes frilled edges, it's probably a moon snail egg case or "collar" as it's sometimes called. Each is filled with thousands of eggs, mixed with sand and held together with mucus. When the eggs hatch, the case disintegrates.

SCOTCH BONNET

Beneath the rough surf of North Carolina's Outer Banks lie the Diamond Shoals, shifting sandbars that have smashed hundreds of ships since the colonial era. Here at Cape Hatteras, where the southern Florida and northern Labrador currents meet, a wide range of Atlantic sea life mingles, including the scotch bonnet snail that makes its home among the ships' wreckage.

With its crisscrossing fine lines that resemble a textile's weave and its patches of orange, the surface of the scotch bonnet is the tartan plaid of the sea, named in honor of North Carolina's Scottish settlers. Formally, the texture is referred to as *nodulose* (granulated). Its other defining characteristics are its disproportionately large first whorl, and its thick lip with distinct *lirae* (ridges).

It's a rare shell now; finding one is equivalent to snagging a junonia on Sanibel, which sports similar spots but is much less fragile and doesn't bleach as easily in the sun. The scotch bonnet's more ephemeral nature makes it, perhaps, even more of a find. The hurricanes and tropical storms that so often damage the Outer Banks offer these shells on shore as a consolation to local shellers.

Streets along North Carolina's coast are named in honor of the scotch bonnet; it was also the first state shell in the country—the North Carolina Shell Club initiated the bill, which became law in 1965. A number of other coastal states followed suit by naming their own state shells, including the lettered olive, oyster, northern quahog, scallop, and more.

WENTLETRAP

In the early days of European natural curiosity collecting, wentletraps were coveted for their graceful forms and rarity. Cosimo di Giovanni de' Medici, who knew a thing or two about beauty given his patronage of Renaissance artists Fra Angelico, Fra Filippo Lippi, and Donatello, owned a wentletrap. Later, Holy Roman Emperor Francis I and Catherine the Great of Russia included the prized specimens in their cabinets. The obsessive collection of rare shells in this seafaring era was known as *conchylomania*.

Wentletrap snails inhabit all of the oceans, from the tropics to the frigid polar zones, so while they look delicate, they can withstand a range of conditions. The architecture of their white, tan, and ivory shells, with vertical ribs (or *varices*—axial ridges) along the swelled and swirling whorls, quite prominent in some species, might bring to mind a cathedral's carved stone. The name itself is Dutch for "winding staircase." Some liken its design to a turret, which the shell resembles when it's sitting atop its snail.

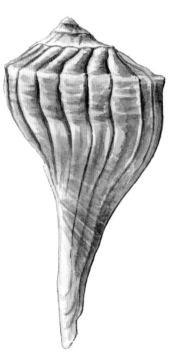

lightning whelk

channeled whelk with egg casing

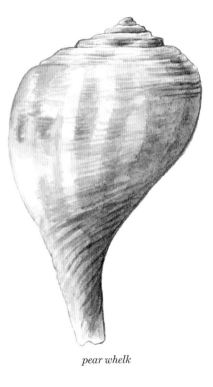

pear whelk

WHELK

That twisty curiosity on the beach that looks like something between a spine and a bumpy snakeskin is actually a strand of whelk egg casings. After a whelk lays the string of podlike cases, it anchors one end of the chain into the sand to keep the eggs underwater. The eggs inside each case are surrounded by a sort of amniotic gel; out of each of these 40 to 160 pods will come 40 or more tiny whelks in their perfectly formed shells.

Knobbed and lightning whelks lay egg cases with ridged edges, while the channeled whelk's case sides are fused together around the edge and have a sort of sunburst set of ridges on the fronts and backs. Pear whelk capsules have spiky edges. The egg casings of horse conchs have a similar color and structure, but the capsules are triangular rather than oval and are clustered rather than set individually in a curling row. If you find these "mermaid's necklaces" on the beach and the capsules are dried out and sound like a rattle, the juveniles didn't make it. But if the cases are still squishy, if the gel is still intact, they might have a chance, so do nature a favor and toss them back over the surf line.

Whelks are fierce snails that fish for dinner by wrapping their foot around bivalves, pulling the two valves apart, and wedging them open further with the sharp lip of their own shells. Many coastal communities, in turn, eat whelks, whether skewered, in stews, or served in their shells with garlic butter and parsley. There are fifty species, including the state shell of Massachusetts, the wrinkled whelk.

MORE GORGEOUS GASTROPODS

From the spherical turban shell to the swirling banded tulip, from the glassy, elongated olive to the textured murex, aquatic snails exhibit an astonishing capacity for design solutions—they're architects of the sea, designing and building their magnificent homes.

Their construction method, like that of the bivalves, is a deceptively simple one: accretion. As they outgrow their shells, they secrete a calcium carbonate- and protein-rich fluid through tubes in their flesh along the outside edge of their apertures. The fluid hardens to become the youngest part of the shell. How mollusks produce the colors in their shells is not yet completely understood, nor is how such a lowly form of life can be so brilliantly programmed to create unique patterns and forms over their lifetime, and from generation to generation.

Marine zoologists who research these mysteries mention phenotypes, phylogeny, sigmoid responses, and logarithmic spirals to describe their observations, which are beyond the ken of us average beachcombers. But, we all share the sense of wonder for and appreciation of the beautiful objects that the sea holds, then shares.

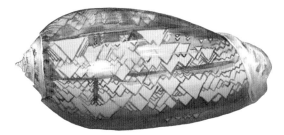

tent olive

crown turban

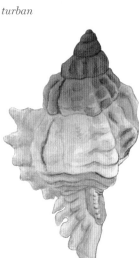

rose murex

banded tulip

Echinoderms, Crustaceans, and Other Beach Treasures

Occasionally, something of empiric value is tossed by the waves, exposed by them—or even floated down to them from inland shores. Along a 200-mile [320-km] stretch of Namibia's coast, some of the world's costliest diamonds that traveled along South Africa's Orange River are deposited, polished by the sand and sea, and thrown back onto the beach. But most of us are happy just to find our shells, beautiful pieces of sea-sanded glass, and other collectibles like children's toys, and, if we're lucky, something really special like an arrowhead or a message in a bottle.

Some of the most fascinating things we find are the former homes of *echinoderms*, a 6,000-member phylum that includes sea stars, sand dollars, and sea urchins. All of the creatures in this group are radially symmetric: their appendages and *tests* (the hard endoskeleton surrounding sand dollars and urchins) are designed from the center out like spokes of a wheel, usually in *pentamerous* sets (five sections). Some members of the urchin family have spines that can be rotated toward predators on ball joints; sand dollars' (a type of urchin) spines are short and number in the thousands, covering the surface of live specimens with a kind of velvety texture. Echinoderms are colonial, living together in large populations, which is why you can often find them together on the beach after they're stranded by storms. These animals all use an *aquatic vascular system*, taking in and expelling seawater to fuel their locomotion with sets of tube feet.

The shells of crustaceans, like lobsters, shrimp, and crabs, are actually *exoskeletons* (as opposed to our inner skeletons), which the animals, like the insects they're related to, molt as they grow, unlike mollusks that add to the shells they're born with. There are roughly 67,000 species of crustaceans in the oceans and seas; the fossil records for some dates back to the Triassic period. Barnacles are crustaceans, too, but are *sessile* (stationary), with no means to move once they hunker down on hard surfaces. The pieces of crabs that we find most often on the beach, the top or dorsal section of their shells that look a little like lids, are called *carapaces*. With their varieties of spots and colors and shapes, these, too, make interesting additions to a beachcomber's collection.

SAND DOLLAR

When you look out to sea, you probably don't picture thousands of sand dollars below the surface that have anchored themselves at 90-degree angles on the ocean floor, feeding on tasty bits that currents bring their way, as some species do. When they're not standing on their edges, sand dollars also burrow into the sand using their bristly tube feet. Much like sea stars, sand dollars are viewed by many beachcombers as mere decorative objects, but they were indeed living animals before they washed ashore—creatures that have been around in their basic form for sixty-six million years.

Sand dollars are essentially flat sea urchins. However, certain types, like sea biscuits and heart urchins, are puffy as if inflated, more closely resembling their fully rounded cousins that we simply call "urchins." Like their cousins, sand dollars have fairly complex five-piece jaws that are moved by some sixty muscles. These pieces resemble little birds, found when the shell (or *test*, as urchins' casings are properly called), breaks open; some refer to them as "peace doves," or in some Spanish-speaking locales, *angelitas*—little angels.

On Georgia's pristine Little St. Simons Island, I once found hundreds of purple keyhole sand dollars. There's something wonderful about finding too many to count, the feeling of a healthy community beneath the waves. Take care when you find

{continued}

keyhole sand dollar

these, though: if they're still colorful and have a sort of velvet feel, or if their feet are moving, they're still alive. Beyond not wanting to take an animal from its environment, you won't want to get hit with the hefty fines that some places impose on those who take living creatures from the beach— nor get whacked with the punishing smell when you pack them! To be safe, take only those that are white from sand abrasion and sun bleaching, and be especially cautious about how you pack them for the journey home (see page 122 for more information).

Ah! what pleasant visions haunt me

As I gaze upon the sea!

All the old romantic legends,

All my dreams, come back to me.

— HENRY WADSWORTH LONGFELLOW

SEA STAR

Of all the treasures found on island and mainland beaches, sea stars (commonly known as starfish) are among the most fascinating. They're not "fish" at all—they're echinoderms, kin to sea urchins and sand dollars, hence the recent reidentification campaign to change the name to "sea stars" for all two thousand species. For many of us, stars are most commonly seen when used in beachy craft projects long after they've expired—but in reality, they're some of the most elegant predators in the seas.

Stars are effective, if slow-moving, hunters, gripping urchins and other prey and prying open their shells to eat them. Their benign looks belie a fierce nature. They pull clamped shells apart, then evert their stomachs around the flesh of their victim and pull it all back inside. One mussel is a day's sustenance for an average star. According to Dr. David Pawson, emeritus senior scientist at the Smithsonian's National Museum of Natural History, until a few years ago it was believed that the tube feet that line their arms would stick onto clams, mussels, and rocks like suction cups. But Belgian scientists recently discovered that the feet have two sets of glands: one set squirts a glue-like substance that instantly sticks the feet to the surface, and then the second set squirts an "antidote," which counteracts the instant glue. This quick-stick and quick-release adhesive technique is now being studied for industrial and medical applications.

{continued}

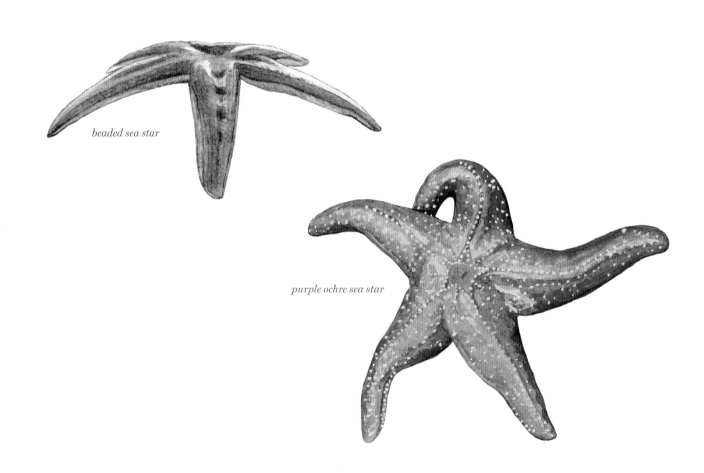

beaded sea star

purple ochre sea star

Stars use their surprising agility to "walk," slowly, in an undulating motion back to the sea on their five arms with their bodies lifted. They do the same to turn themselves over in a move that looks a lot like yoga. And similar to some species of lizards that can regrow their tails, sea stars can regenerate their arms.

One of my favorite island moments involved sea stars. As I approached the ocean through the scrub brush in the dark before sunrise, I could see star silhouettes spangling the beach, with eighty-five counted in just a 100-yard [91-m] stretch. There was something spectacular about seeing them all, dark against light sand, beneath the light-against-inky-sky stars overhead, as if those on the beach had fallen from the sky.

Sea stars come in a wide range of colors and shapes, some with many more than five arms. On Puget Sound beaches in Washington State, purple and orange ochres stretch across the pebbles. Ochres are comical stars—puffy and beaded as if they're wearing jewelry; the species was used as reference for Peach in *Finding Nemo*. They can grow up to 10 inches [25 cm] across, weigh up to 1 pound [455 g] and can live for twenty years.

A CAST OF CRABS

For Marylanders, learning how to pick steamed crabs is part of native training; we figure they're fair game since they pinch our toes when we wade into the water, plus, they're delicious! The blue crab's scientific name, *Callinectes sapidus*, means "savory beautiful swimmer," and indeed their olive green bodies and bright cerulean claws (called "chela")—which in females or "sooks" have red-tipped pincers as if they'd been to the salon— are lovely. Along the mid-Atlantic coast (although they're also in the Gulf of Mexico), the blue crab is a symbol of summer.

There are thousands of marine crab species, from the ¼ inch [6 mm] pea crab that holes up inside bivalves like oysters to the Japanese spider crab with a length of up to 13 feet [4 m]. Their relatives have populated the earth since the Jurassic period. Groups of crabs are known as a cast, with some species' members communicating with one another by drumming or waving their claws. Scavenging omnivores, they've been known to work together to feed the group, but they're also scrappy fighters, stepping into the ring over mates and places to hide, pinching and kicking with all ten of their legs.

{continued}

shore crab

blue crab

mottled purse crab

Varieties found on Atlantic beaches besides the blue crab include the fiddler, ghost, and mottled purse crabs. Pretty little purple to red shore crabs scamper over the pebbled Pacific Northwest beaches, where you'll also sometimes find small Dungeness crabs. It's common to come across just carapaces—crabs' "lids," so seeing one with all its parts intact is special. If you find one you'd like for your collection, make sure it's thoroughly sundried, or the smell will be terrible. Their limbs are fragile at the joints to the body, and can break off pretty easily, so keep them separated from the rest of your shells as you stroll and pack them separately for transport home if you're on vacation (see page 122 for tips).

I started Early – Took my Dog –
And visited the Sea –
The Mermaids in the Basement
Came out to look at me –

— EMILY DICKINSON

BARNACLE

You might overlook barnacles on beach walks, thinking only of how their encrustation on boat hulls earned them the nickname "crusty foulers" and of how unsightly they are on dock pilings. Although they look primitive—seemingly far, far down the sentient being chain—their unremarkable looks belie an unsurpassed method of attaching to marine surfaces, and in one species, the goose-neck barnacle, a delicacy, according to coastal residents of Spain and the Pacific Northwest, with meat that's said to be as sweet as lobster.

Although they look like mollusks, barnacles are in fact crustaceans; most have carapaces made of *chitin* (a material similar to fingernails' keratin), like those of lobsters and crabs and insect exoskeletons, which they, too, outgrow and shed. They also sport antennae and have segmented bodies like their shrimp and lobster cousins.

There are well over a thousand kinds of barnacles in the world's waters. Most species develop their hard shells once they've attached to surfaces and a number are specialized, living only on certain creatures like whales, sea turtles, and crabs. They can be fairly choosy about their abodes, feeling surfaces out; if a substrate is deemed substandard, they'll detach and float back out into the current to find a better spot. When they do find their dream home, they secrete first an oily substance onto the surface that repels the water, then an adhesive that permanently attaches them; these secretions are being studied for use in dentistry.

{continued}

Even though they're hermaphrodites, they have to cozy up to their neighbors to reproduce. They live five to ten years, if shorebirds or crabs don't snack on them.

So the next time you're bent over looking for seaside treasure, don't be so quick to dismiss the barnacle. Acorn barnacle carapaces are pretty, with deep pink streaks; they can be a nice element in collections. They have six neatly fitted plates that enclose four more plates, which serve as a trapdoor. When the tide is out, they close to keep moisture in; when the tide is in, they open, allowing the barnacles' feathery appendages, called *cirri*, to catch plankton and other sources of food as they float by. These are accomplished crustaceans.

SEA URCHIN

My first sea urchin test—the proper name for this creature's shell—was waiting for me at Arniston in South Africa, where the aqua Indian and blue-gray Atlantic oceans meet at the bottom tip of the continent. The bright green Cape sea urchins are a happy spot of color, and their delicate structures are unlikely surf survivors, so they're extra-special gifts when found whole. I've found urchins since on Tybee Island, Georgia, and on Florida islands including Cook's, Key West, and Captiva, and each time, I'm thrilled by the discovery.

The creatures, which live in colonies by the thousands, are nicknamed the "porcupines of the sea" because of their spines, which are both their armor and a means of locomotion across the sea floor, along with their tube feet. A colony's collective "spine canopy" shelters juvenile urchins and abalone as well as shrimp and other fish from predators.

Urchins have five strong, curved, pointed teeth that can bore through rock and through their regular meals of kelp and various invertebrates. The teeth open outward and chomp down and around, like the claw in arcade prize machines.

But even with spiked surfaces and effective teeth, urchins can't compete against fishermen (who supply sushi chefs), lobsters, and sea otters. Otters break off the spines with their paws, chomp down through the delicate shell, and eat the insides.

If you're fortunate enough to find an empty test from the more than two hundred species of urchins, whether green, purple, or other colors, make sure you take care with wrapping and packing them, with lots of cotton batting or bubble wrap inside a nice firm box (or a shoe, in a pinch).

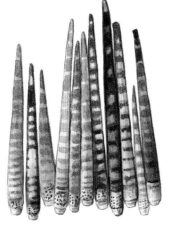

lance urchin spines

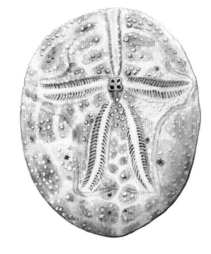

heart urchin

underside of purple sea urchin
(showing teeth)

HORSESHOE CRAB

Horseshoe crabs are common along America's Atlantic coast and can be seen in the hundreds of thousands when they migrate to Delaware's shores in late spring. If you've ever come across one turned over on its back, you've seen the squirming-leg family resemblance that crustaceans share. But despite their name and crab resemblance, horseshoes are more closely related to spiders and scorpions, and aren't crabs at all. Like dragonflies and gingko trees, horseshoe crabs are referred to as living fossils, as their design has remained essentially unchanged for some 445 million years.

While they might look a little dangerous with their spiky *telson*, a daggerlike body part, they're harmless to humans. They use the telson to turn themselves back over when flipped upside down. Not only are they harmless, they actually help us with their copper-rich blue blood; it contains an amino acid that coagulates in the presence of bacterial toxins, so hospitals use it to detect bacteria on surfaces, as do astronauts on the International Space Station. They also aid shorebird populations; their eggs account for as much as 50 percent of the diets of red knots and other birds.

Horseshoe crabs molt many times when they're young and growing, so you might find their shed shells on the beach. When they're small, the shells can be almost like paper. These are fragile, so take extra care when packing them (see page 122 for more details).

SKATE EGG CASE

Among the more curious natural objects found on beaches around the world are egg cases—home to the growing pups of some species of skates, dogfish, and sharks (as well as whelks, tulips, and horse conchs). While many of these creatures give birth to live young, almost half of them lay eggs surrounded by these oddly shaped cases with horns on each corner. The cases themselves are made of collagen and keratin, like our fingernails; the horns have gummy surfaces that help them to stay anchored on seaweeds or grasses. They're nicknamed "mermaid's purses" in many beach communities.

When a skate pup hatches, it wriggles out of its pouch and swims free by flapping its newly unfolded wings. It's like a butterfly unfurling from its cocoon and taking to the skies. The case itself is eventually pulled away from the grasses during storms and floats to shore, where beachcombers find it in the wrack line. If you pick one up but it feels like maybe someone is still home—if you don't see that the case has been opened between the horns and it still feels supple—hold it up to the light to see if there's a form inside. If so, toss it back in the water to give it a chance to hatch.

If you're visiting Florida's Gulf Coast, you might try the "Sanibel shuffle": scuffing along the sand below the surf to let burrowed skates know you're coming so you don't step on them.

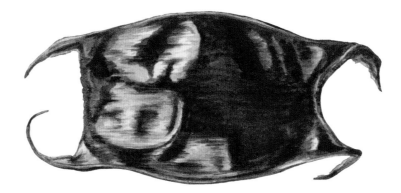

SEA BEAN

I've visited more than one hundred American islands and other mainland and international beaches, but I'd never heard of sea beans—the colloquial term for beached seeds from a host of mainly tropical plants—before Tony Reisinger, marine biologist and beachcomber extraordinaire, pointed them out a couple years ago, tangled in the sargassum seaweed wrack on South Padre Island in Texas. It's funny how beachcombers' eyes are trained to spot different shapes on the beach—how some people find sharks' teeth, others find certain shells (my specialty is baby's ears), and still others find things like sea glass shards or sea beans, while others pass them by.

A week after my introduction, I saw a bowlful of the beans in a Key West, Florida, shop, where they were presented as "lucky." What I know now is that sea bean enthusiasts have a website (www.seabean.com) with a newsletter, *The Drifting Seed*, that's distributed to people in twenty countries; a number of books have been written on the subject; and that there's an annual Sea-Bean Symposium in the fall where "bean-a-thoners" gather and compete for the Cool Bean Award. In Brevard County, Florida, a "Drifters" group is dedicated to all the "corkies" (rough-surfaced seeds) and "shiners" (smooth-surfaced seeds).

There are more than two hundred kinds of sea beans landing on Florida's eastern shores alone. But, of course, they're found all over the world, both in their original homes and on the coastlines where they land. Air pockets and light, corky construction keep them afloat, while hard shells make them waterproof as they journey thousands of miles. They can spend years surfing the currents before finally stranding, and some can

{continued}

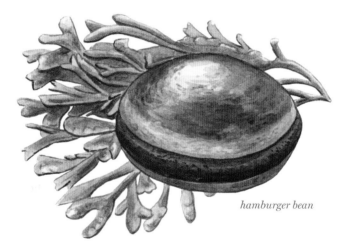

hamburger bean

remain viable as plants for as many as ten years. Because of their buoyancy, they're often found at the high-tide line mixed in with seaweed and reeds.

The South Atlantic equatorial current brings nicker nuts, sea purses, true sea beans (a.k.a. hamburger beans), and sea hearts to southeast American beaches. The Gulf Stream carries Jamaican navel spurges, deer eyes, and others from South America and the Caribbean (where some are called jumbie beads) to southeastern shores (easiest to find on the eastern Florida coast in September and October, and along the Texas Gulf coast in March, April, and May), carrying them onward to Ireland and points beyond if they don't come ashore in North America. On Costa Rica's Pacific coast, an hour-long walk can yield hundreds of seeds. Enthusiasts have "Holy Grail" beans on their life lists. Here are a few varieties:

The true sea bean is carried by some Africans as a charm against illness; in Mexico (where it's referred to as an *ojo de venado*, or deer's eye), it's used in children's bracelets, engraved with saints, as a protection from the evil eye. I've heard that older Floridians carry them in their pockets for luck.

Gray nicker nuts have been used as talismans, sometimes set in sterling silver crosses. They're called *airne moire* in Gaelic—the Virgin's charm of deliverance. According to a nineteenth-century volume on Gaelic incantations, they were carried by midwives in the Outer Hebrides, who had women in labor clutch them in their right hands and recite the Ave Maria three times to "to release the child and succor the woman." As they did this, the midwives walked in a circle around the mother-to-be, praying. Children would wear the amulet around their necks to protect them from witchcraft. Some historians say that the seedpod was from a Jamaican macuna, landing on Orkney's shores, or perhaps it comes from the sea heart from monkey ladder seeds. Mary's beans, the mother plant of which is the morning glory family of vines, are said to hold similar powers—they have a shallow cross shape on one side, and on the other, an indentation design that people liken to a baby in utero. Sea hearts are also considered good luck charms; among the larger of the seeds, they're sometimes polished and engraved, like cameos.

Other seeds have curious names including brainfruit, candlenut, antidote vine, porcupine seed, railroad vine, and bloodwood, and there's the deep-red Cathie's bean, named in honor of Cathie Katz, who founded *The Drifting Seed* newsletter and Sea-Bean Symposium.

Cleaning the seeds is generally easy with soap and water or a little alcohol, but some will improve with a gentle sanding to remove bristly "hairs." Some people put a bit of wax or coconut oil on them, or use a rotary tool with a polishing wire-brush head and then shine them up with mineral oil.

Soon after that day on South Padre Island, Tony gave me a protective deer eye (*ojo de venado*) bean from his collection during a time when I needed a little help from a friend. I like to think of it as my good luck charm, as I'm *almost* as much of a vagabond as the seeds are; it also reminds me to remain buoyant in even the most trying tempests. Mainly, though, it reminds me of a happy day on a beautiful beach with a fellow beachcomber.

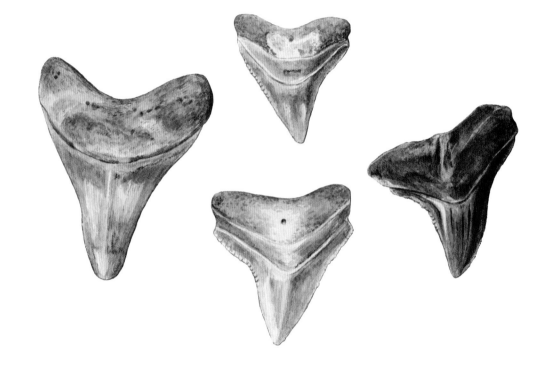

SHARK TOOTH

Since sharks have been swimming the seas for hundreds of millions of years, and since many coastlines used to be underwater, and because sharks have multiple rows of teeth, losing hundreds daily (and using up to thirty thousand in their lifetimes)—well, it's basic math: there are lots of their teeth to be found. A single dead shark can leave thousands of teeth deposited in one spot on the sea floor.

Gradually, over thousands of years, the lost dentine and enamel are replaced by the minerals in the sand or sediment, so many sharks' teeth found by beachcombers are actually shark tooth–shaped fossils, some of which are as big as your hand. A single megalodon tooth can be 7 inches [17 cm] long and can fetch thousands at auction. There are certain spots, like Venice, Florida (which sits on top of a deep fossil layer), where you're more likely to find shark teeth. People use sifters in these locations to more easily find them; sandbars tend to be lucky spots.

Different sharks have different teeth, depending on their diet. Fish eaters have long, needled teeth, while whale sharks, those gentle giants, have almost decorative teeth, as they eat mainly plankton, which don't require chewing. Great white and bull sharks have serrated teeth that help them bite off big chunks of prey. Some shark teeth are so sharp that they were used as carving tools in Polynesian cultures; they're believed to have been used to create glyphs on driftwood *rongorongo* tablets on Easter Island, which have yet to be translated. No matter what kind of teeth you find, they make a good addition to a well-rounded beachcombing collection.

ARROWHEAD

Native Americans have lived along our shorelines for thousands of years, in summer fishing camps or year-round homes, or operating as traders with other tribes along the coasts. The Calusa of southern Florida used shells for a variety of tools, including hoes fashioned from conchs as well as stone spearheads for fishing and hunting. Today lucky beachcombers can find the rare arrowhead or spearhead—*points*, as collectors call them—most of which are made from locally sourced quartz; less common are arrowheads made from jasper, flint, or chert. One of the interesting aspects of finding an arrowhead is that the type of stone will tell you how far it traveled back in its day—the material is a clue to the tool's origin, revealing tribal trade routes.

On Smith Island, Maryland, in the Chesapeake Bay, surface hunters have found thousands of points, picking up what nature exposed to this crabbing community. One find by Tim Marshall, an Eppes Island, Virginia, spear point, dates from the Ice Age era of mammoths and saber-toothed tigers (about twelve thousand years before Captain John Smith's arrival). When you think about a hunter facing off against those immense animals, hurling these points tied to the ends of wooden rods—when you hold the arrowhead that he shaped with antler points, chipping and flaking the stone into the weapon, you connect to history in a unique way.

On New York's Shelter Island, John Pagliaro has found hundreds of arrowheads. Some are

{continued}

jasper Susquehanna broad point

"heartbreakers" that are damaged in some way, which he incorporates into jewelry designs for his gallery, but others are as they were when in use by Manhasset Indians. Some are a smoky quartz while others are veined, clear, or tinged with rose. Long Island varieties include Agate Basin, Dalton, Lamoka, Taconic stemmed, Squibnocket, and many more.

Points have been found at the Jersey Shore, on South Carolina's Edisto Island, along Puget Sound and the Gulf of Mexico's beaches, and many more coastal (as well as inland) locations. My grandfather found them around Maryland's western shore. If you do "go rockin'," pay attention to local antiquities laws to avoid fines for taking archeological resources, especially on public lands.

I could never stay long enough on the shore; the tang of the untainted, fresh, and free sea air was like a cool, quieting thought.

— HELEN KELLER

SEA GLASS

There's something about a beach gleaming with frosted sea glass that's pure magic—as if nature lifted the lid of an ancient pirate's trunk to reveal a wealth of jewels. In a few spots around the world, there are so many ocean-smoothed shards that they clink against each other while tumbling toward shore. It's a kind of homecoming celebration, given that glass is made from sand.

Sea glassers, like all collectors, have their bucket lists. Among the most sought-after pieces are red shards. Red glass was originally made with gold additives, making it costly. There have been few commercial uses for red glass, so it's rare—most is thought to come from old boat port lights or vintage car backup lights. Also on the scarce side are glass stoppers (like you'd find in perfume bottles or decanters), marbles, and what are called "end of days"—items that were either tossed out as waste by bottle factory workers, or more fanciful shapes that were practice pieces made after the close of business.

Cobalt-blue glass from old pharmacy bottles is desirable, as are *multis*—pieces with layered colors—but really anything well "cooked" by the sea's combination of waves, rocks, and sand is a win. There are charts that show what's commonly found (white, brown, and beer-bottle green varieties) and what are considered real coups: purples, yellows, oranges, reds, and blacks, which are usually very dark brown or green. Beyond the colors, experts offer clues to knowing how old your piece might be, including mold marks, bottle lip shapes, and lettering and designs in the glass. Ultimately, each shard of sea glass is a puzzle piece—one

{continued}

whose neighboring pieces won't be found to reveal the whole, so it takes some detective work to figure it out.

The majority of shards come from glass bottles (*vessel glass* to insiders), so the beaches with the highest concentration of sea glass are near what once were dumps (Glass Beach at Fort Bragg, California, and the beach at Spectacle Island, Massachusetts—both "look but don't take" locations; Dead Horse Bay in Brooklyn, New York; Bermuda's Dockyard Beach) or glass manufacturers (Seaham in England, near what was the Londonderry Bottleworks—England's largest in Victorian times). Beaches near dangerous shoals where ships wrecked frequently, the Great Lakes' shores, and Puerto Rico's sands are also known to be good hunting grounds.

If you're tempted to buy sea glass, be advised that much is made overseas by smashing bottles and putting the shards in rock tumblers to get the look. You can tell these fake pieces apart from genuine sea glass by their uniform frosting and textures; most are missing telltale "C" indentations from chinking against rocks and shells often found on genuine sea glass, although counterfeiters are now including these as well to increase the value of their wares.

CLAY BABY

On Fox Island in Washington's Puget Sound, beach-combers are less interested in collecting shells, rocks, or sea stars as others do on the more than four hundred islands in the state; the objects of their attention are seaside anomalies called *clay babies*.

Clay babies are a unique feature of Fox Island: an open vein of clay seeps out into the sea and is "cured"—broken off, hardened, and tumbled—by the saltwater and sun into fantastical shapes, some of which loosely resemble miniature human forms. Many more take on animal shapes like seals and rabbits. Considering these figures is akin to seeing shapes in clouds—much is open to inter-pretive whim. It takes a trained eye to spot these on the pebbled shore; locals who have decades of experience finding them refer to one secret area as their "nursery," where the water meets the clay to begin forming the concretions.

In the 1930s, Works Progress Administration (WPA) writer Alfred J. Smith included "The Legend of the Mud Babies" in his *Along the Waterfront* work. There are a variety of local legends, includ-ing those from the Coast Salish tribe of the area, usually involving an earth maiden who falls in love with a merman. Once the maiden transforms into a mermaid, she leaves the shapes on shore as a message of her well-being for her family. As rare as these clay creatures are, it's no wonder that they'd take on mythic qualities.

Much of Fox Island is private property; many street signs indicate as much, so keep this in mind when you're walking to get to the beach. Use des-ignated access points only.

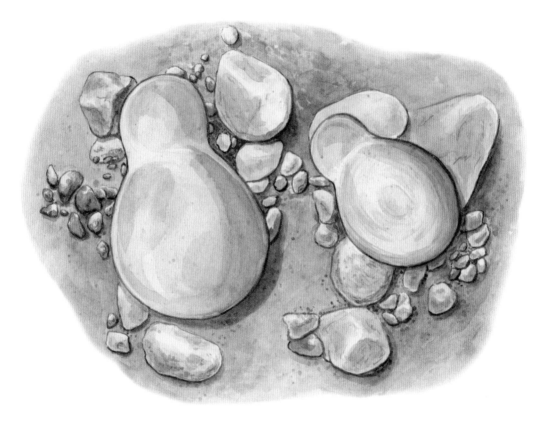

TOYS, SHOES, AND OTHER FLOTSAM

On any given day seashells, driftwood, sea beans, or random manmade items including sunglasses, flasks, lures, and toys make their way to shore. You can't predict what'll be tossed onto your path at the beach, and every now and again, the surf kicks up something that's more than simply interesting or beautiful—something that seems to be a kind of message. Many beachcombers believe in the sea's ability to deliver meaningful objects at crucial times.

Sandy West tells the story of how in the 1970s, when she was negotiating the terms of sale for Ossabaw—the wild barrier island her parents had purchased for their winter home—to the State of Georgia, she walked along Boneyard Beach to clear her head after a particularly contentious round. She stumbled upon a small plastic boxing glove in the foam, which she says instantly renewed her vigor. In a "What are the odds?" moment fifty years later, during another series of confrontations with the state to preserve what had been agreed upon a half century before, she found an identical plastic boxing glove on another of the island's beaches—exactly the same, save the color—and again her strength was bolstered. She keeps them both in a fabric bag on her bedpost as a reminder to fight the good fight.

I've heard other stories of people finding eyeglasses at a moment when they needed to "see" something differently, or an action figure when they felt called to be heroic. While most objects don't roll in as talismans from the deep, there are those random manmade pieces that can come to good use. Some make wreaths from the fishing bobs and doll parts they find along beaches; others tack the shoes, goggles, and other bits onto their fences as decoration. One person's trash is indeed another's treasure.

MESSAGE IN A BOTTLE

People have tossed bottled messages into rivers and oceans since at least the third century B.C.—not long after glass vessels and paper were invented. But even now, optimists cast their ideas and hopes into the water. It doesn't matter that there's email and airmail; the point isn't sending it to someone you know, even if they're the inspiration for the writing, but to an unknown recipient. Message-in-a-bottle hunter Clint Buffington has walked countless sandy miles to find more than eighty bottles that fall into common genres including scientific studies ("drift" bottles cast by oceanographers studying currents or by fisheries' marine biologists), pen pal requests, love letters, eulogies (including cremated remains), and hoaxes ("I'm being held against my will" is a common theme here). The tricky part, he says, is extracting the sometimes wet paper without tearing it; the best part is the sense of connectivity to strangers around the globe, who sent their bottles out as many as fifty years ago.

My favorite message-in-a-bottle story comes from Ossabaw Island in Georgia. Many decades ago while walking along Boneyard Beach with her young son, the island's owner, Sandy West, found a bottle with a message. Because her daughter wasn't with them, Sandy insisted that they wait until dinnertime to open the bottle as a family. Her son's hours of brutal waiting only became more painful when he was finally allowed to uncork the bottle and take the paper out. He was too young to read, so handed it to Sandy, who burst out laughing at the note—but wouldn't tell the children why: there were only two words on the paper—a decidedly unromantic expletive.

PART TWO

A Beachcomber's Tool Kit

The Beachcomber's Commandments

We've all heard the admonition "take only pictures, leave only footprints," but beachcombers are collectors by nature—we want to take at least a few shells, or an interesting pebble, or a piece of driftwood home with us. Still, there are basic rules of respectful behavior—and common sense—that should be observed. As beachcombers, we're called to be beach stewards, too; it's part of the creed.

1. Never, ever take a live creature or plant from the beach. If you return to your cottage and realize there's someone home in that shell, or that your child has collected a live sea star (you can tell by their limbs going a bit limp when you lift them, and see their "feet" moving on their underside), sand dollar (ditto, and they won't be bright white, but rather purple or brown), or sea urchin or snail (their "trapdoor" operculum will be in place over the shell's opening, meaning the snail retreated into its home), return the creature immediately to the ocean. Don't wait until the next morning or put them in tap water. Many localities have laws that forbid taking live animals from beaches and out a ½ mile [805 m] off of shore. There's also a Convention on International Trade in Endangered Species of Wild Fauna and Flora that prohibits taking certain shells out of some countries—you may have your prizes confiscated at the airport or on the cruise ship.

In addition, there are a number of beaches that prohibit taking any shells or sea glass, while others impose limits on how many shells each person can take. Other beaches are closed at times because of nesting birds. Make sure you know the rules before you become attached to something you can't keep.

2. If you see an animal in distress, don't interfere. As pure as your intentions may be, you can cause a distressed creature more harm than good. Alert a lifeguard, or contact a park ranger or police officer, if possible. Many coastal towns have marine centers and wild animal refuges that might be able to help. A number of states offer training for civilians interested in becoming beach stewards; check in your area so you can learn to better assist. All of this said, there's nothing wrong with repatriating a horseshoe crab or whatever you've found back into the water if the tide has left it behind. Just be sure to place the creatures in the water; do not throw them as that can shock their systems or injure them.

3. Tempting as it is to interact with wild creatures, don't feed them or otherwise disturb their natural behaviors. Observe, but resist engaging. You might find yourself being dive-bombed by a hungry flock of birds, having a wild horse charge you if you get too close to a foal, or being bitten by something you thought was just going to make a great picture or story to tell your friends. Try to stay at least a school-bus length away from anything wild.

4. Stick to clear, designated paths to avoid trampling dune grasses or disturbing nests. This is also for your own safety. On one of Florida's more remote Gulf coast islands, I went off the trail in my flip-flops through a few yards of leaf litter to get a photograph of a white ibis. I found out thirty minutes later, from a kind exterminator, that the island is full of scorpions. I'd been told to stay on the paths, but no one said anything about vermin; I thought it was more to preserve the landscaping.

5. Respect private property. In many areas, homeowners' properties extend to the high-tide mark on the beach. Don't trespass on their lawns, even though they look like public beaches. Stay within the low- and high-tide zone known as the littoral. And don't cut through peoples' properties to get to beaches.

6. Be selective about the shells you take home as souvenirs. Remember that if everyone took as many shells as you've sometimes picked up, far fewer people could enjoy their shelling experiences. Even in places that don't impose limits, sometimes locals rely on the wash-ashore treasures for their livelihoods. As Anne Morrow Lindbergh wrote in *Gift from the Sea* (a book based on her two-week solo holiday on Captiva Island in Florida): "The sea does not reward those who are too anxious, too greedy, or too impatient." No hoarding!

7. Carry a separate trash bag with you to pick up the odd bit of garbage or broken glass you might come across. And of course, clean up after yourself, disposing of all trash appropriately. A number of beaches are also banning plastic bags and balloons, because these go out to sea where turtles and other creatures mistake them for something edible like jellyfish, only to end up with trash filling their bellies. In short, try to leave the beach cleaner than you found it.

8. Take precautions during night shelling. Don't go in the water farther than up to your ankles; you might not be able to see things you should

Go gather by the humming sea

Some twisted, echo-harboring shell,

And to its lips thy story tell,

And they thy comforters will be

— WILLIAM BUTLER YEATS

avoid, like sharks and rays. Look out for turtles and their tracks while you make your way in low light; nesting areas for turtles and birds are usually roped off, but if they're waddling toward the water they might be outside the ropes. If it's egg-hatching season, cover your flashlight or lantern with a red plastic film so the little guys don't get confused by the light (they don't see red light), and don't leave any beach-facing lights on at your cottage or condo. Mark the site on the beach where you came off a path; in the dark, it's very difficult to tell one stretch of beach from another—a simple stack of driftwood or some other sign will do. Be sure to wear shoes since you can't see as well, and watch where you're walking. Holes dug for sandcastles can land you in the hospital with a broken ankle.

9. Respect the ocean's dangers. Seas are full of beautiful but dangerous animals that would just as soon sting, bite, or poison you as delight you. If you don't know what something is, don't approach it, and if it can eat you, try not to bring attention to yourself. Even innocuous-looking blobs like jellyfish can pack a venomous or at least painful punch, and some cone snails, pretty and innocent as their shells appear, can send a deadly harpoon into you.

Remember how powerful and unpredictable the sea is. When the tide goes out, it's tempting to go farther and farther to look for shells, but there are places where the tide can visibly rush back at you. And pay attention to lifeguard flags. They aren't just for swimmers; even when you're wading in to look for shells, the surf's backwash can knock you down and get you into trouble. Finally, storm chasers, beware: "When thunder roars, get indoors."

10. Don't be a hero: pack insect repellent. It's a war out there. Biting black flies, carnivorous green flies, mosquitoes, sand gnats ("no-see-ums"), ticks: there are many troops, some stealthier and more dangerous than others, so arm yourself with your weapon of choice.

Be aware of areas with tick populations; walking the paths out to the beach, you'll often pick up blood-sucking hitchhikers on your clothes as you brush by dune grasses or walk over leaf litter. Spray your shoes and socks, not just your skin. You have to be vigilant about looking for even tiny specks, no larger than pieces of ground black pepper. DEET-based sprays are found to be most effective against ticks.

That's what you do to ward off the devils; here's what attracts them in the first place: sweat, standing water, the lactic acid released through your skin after eating spicy food or exercising, scented products like shampoos, lotions, perfume. So, act accordingly.

Cleaning Seashells

When I think back on some of the shells I've left on the beach because they were encrusted with barnacles, or looked chalky white, I could just cry. The die-hard shellers I've come to know in the last years of island hopping have taught me a number of tricks for cleaning and preserving shells that would have made prizes out of those rejects, getting rid of the barnacles and returning the colors you'd think were long gone.

There are a number of ways to give your shells a face-lift. If the "bones" are good—that is, the shell is intact—it's worth the effort to bring out its glory. Shells needing lighter work might respond to a toothpaste and baking soda scrub. For shells that resist gentle attempts at reform, the basic tools for surgery are old clothes and closed-toe shoes; a wire bottle brush; nail- or toothbrush; rubber gloves; goggles; a mask; bleach; muriatic acid* (found in the pool department at hardware stores); a sturdy lidded, handled 5-gallon [19-L] bucket; a bucket of clean water; long tongs; picks (I've used stainless steel nut-picking tools—don't use the sterling silver ones!—but others use dental tools); a metal cuticle pusher; a deep-fryer basket ladle; and mineral oil.

Start off by washing the shells in soapy water to remove dirt, sand, and debris. Use the nail-, bottle-, and toothbrush to clean as much dirt, sand, and debris off and out as possible, and run water through the shell as forcefully as possible.

Tom Eichhorst, editor of *American Conchologist*, says, "Some people use dental ultrasonic baths to get rid of barnacles. I soak shells in a bleach solution, 50 percent bleach, 50 percent water. I remove them every two hours or so and pick at the barnacles. As more come off, the brown stuff from where they attach to the shell remains. So I keep soaking. I use a metal cuticle pusher to remove the barnacle 'skin.' After getting all the brown and barnacles off, I give it a three-second dip in muriatic acid, plunge it in water, then shine it with mineral oil after drying it with a lint-free cloth." Make sure you prepare bleach or muriatic acid soaks in a well-ventilated area. Place the shells in their baths with the tongs or use the fryer ladle to dip them—don't plop them in, as the splashing chemicals could burn you.

When prying off barnacles, use the nut or dental pick to try to work them off from inside, bearing in mind that the lip of some shells can be fragile. Use picks to clean between scallop ridges and whelk and conch spirals, too.

If pieces of the animal remain in the shell, you have a stinky situation on your hands. I've used tweezers to pull out whatever I could, but the stench remained. The consensus seems to be boiling the shell until the last bits float out, and the smell backs off. Other people bury the shell and let insects do their work, then leave the shell

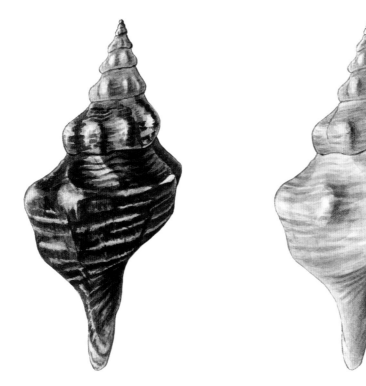

horse conch before cleaning   *horse conch after cleaning*

outside for a while to air out. Still others suggest a vinegar and baking soda bath.

Many suggest that glossy shells like olives, tulips, shark eyes, and cowries should not be left in bleach or acid solutions as they'll dull the shiny finishes. There's a bit of trial and error to all of this; if you're feeling brave, try dipping just for a few seconds first. Other shells' soaking times are dictated by how heavy their *periostracums* (outer coverings) are. Whelks, conchs, clams, and scallops hold up especially well in the baths.

Sand dollars require special care. If you bleach them, only do so for thirty minutes or so. Many people just allow these to bleach in the sun. To strengthen sand dollars after they've been cleaned, coat them in a 50/50 mix of water and regular white glue with a paintbrush. Coat three times, allowing them to dry completely in between.

* *If you use bleach and muriatic acid, make sure you dispose of them carefully. It's okay to put up to a gallon of bleach down your drain, as far as your septic system and pipes go, but keep the water running as it goes. The muriatic acid/water soak needs to be handled differently. It needs to be neutralized, very slowly, with baking soda. Put on the gloves and goggles, then dissolve a pound of baking soda in water in a 3- to 5-gallon [11- to 19-L] plastic bucket. Slowly add the acid water, allowing any fizzing to settle down in between, until the foaming stops. Check with your town or county hazardous waste or sanitation department for specific disposal information.*

The Collector's Travel Kit

Like the old-timers' saying goes, "Shells are where you find them." The beach that was bare yesterday might be covered with shells today, or vice versa. While there are reliable spots ("honey holes" in the vernacular), the ocean giveth, and the ocean taketh away when it comes to shells and other finds. Still, you can better your odds by coming prepared.

So often you see people walking the beach with plastic drinking cups, large quahog shells, or other makeshift containers for collecting treasure. I've been known to tuck my shells into my bathing suit top when I've set off on an impromptu hunting and gathering stroll. But it's easy to put together an inexpensive group of items to help collect and protect your shells so you can keep your hands free on the beach and enjoy your bounty once back home. Here are a few light and small items to pack when you head to the shore:

- a mesh bag, such as those used for washing lingerie (or the larger over-the-shoulder dive bag variety), for collecting

- old pill bottles to keep delicate shells safe and to collect those that might slip through the mesh

- sturdy lidded boxes, such as a plastic travel soap box or leftovers container, to transport delicate shells like urchin tests (in a pinch, I've used the tissue box from the hotel room)

- cotton batting sheets to layer between shells for protection

- sealable sandwich bags for transporting less fragile shells and sand samples

- a fingernail brush for cleaning the shells

- athletic socks for covering larger shells in luggage so they don't snag clothes

Die-hard shellers use specially designed rakes to dig into submerged and exposed shell banks to treasure hunt, but they're tough to pack. Some use nets with long handles, like you might use to dredge leaves out of a pool. Some even use kitty litter scoops! And don't forget to pack water shoes (to protect your feet from sharp shell edges, glass shards, stingrays buried in the sand in shallow water, sea urchin spines, pinching crabs, and so on), a sun-hat, sunscreen, and a pocket knife (don't forget it needs to go in checked bags).

Acknowledgments

I've been a beachcomber since I could walk, but my expertise level on the objects the oceans gift to us is merely that of an amateur. To write this book, I consulted with malacologists and other marine-life specialists including Tom Eichhorst, editor of the quarterly *American Conchologist*; Dr. Jerry Harasewych, Research Zoologist, and Dr. David L. Pawson, emeritus senior scientist, each of the Smithsonian Institution's National Museum of Natural History; and Tony Reisinger, marine biologist with Texas A&M University's Sea Grant Program; Dr. Joseph P. Richardson, emeritus professor of marine sciences, Savannah State University; and the staff (and displays) of the Bailey-Matthews National Shell Museum on Sanibel Island. I'm indebted to all for their responsiveness to my queries and willingness to fact-check sections of the manuscript; any inaccuracies that may remain are entirely my errors.

I also turned to well-informed collectors for assistance. For information on sea glass, I relied upon Lisl Armstrong; for cleaning shells, Donnie Benton and Thomas Robert Campbell; for messages in bottles, Cliff Buffington; for Fox Island's clay babies, Linda Graham; for arrowheads, Tim Marshall and John Pagliaro; for sea beans, Edward L. Perry IV; for wampum history, Berta Welch. Many others, through my *Islands of America* travels as well as shelling clubs and Facebook groups, offered invaluable tried-and-true tips.

A number of collectors kindly permitted us to use photographs of their treasures for illustration references. These include Lisl Armstrong (sea glass); Jennifer Blakeman (imperial Venus); Eric

Heupel (whelk with egg casing); Tammy Steely King (horse conch); Kevin Knutsen (snow buntings); Darynda Kolden (flame auger); Jaclyn Perozze Kraft (juvenile queen conch); Thomas Kupillas (true sea bean and shark teeth); Kim Lincicome (scotch bonnet); Tim Marshall (arrowhead); Ella Maynard (Wedding Cake Venus); Tammy Rahn (rose murex); Deanne Renee (Hawaiian sunrise shell); Troy Schmidt (jingle shells); Sherrie Spangler (clay babies); Doug Stemke (pen shell); Cheryl Meier Vesh (heart urchin); Dawn-Marie Warnick (deer cowrie); and Blair Wright (sea urchin spines). Other shells, objects, and landscapes were drawn mainly from my collection and photographs.

I'm fortunate to have Jillian Ditner as my partner on this project. It's a pleasure to see my words illustrated not only beautifully, but also accurately.

To the hotels from the Atlantic to the Gulf of Mexico to the Pacific that graciously hosted my stays along the coasts, my gratitude: Mansion House Inn, Martha's Vineyard, Massachusetts; Fairfield Inn and Suites, Chincoteague Island, Virginia; The Lodge at Little St. Simons in Georgia; The Island Inn, Sanibel Island, Florida; The Hotel Galvez, Galveston, Texas; Schlitterbahn Beach Resort, South Padre Island, Texas; The Inn at Langley, Whidbey Island, Washington; The Willows Inn, Lummi Island, Washington; Grand Wailea Beach Resort, Maui, Hawaii; Four Seasons Resort Lāna'i Lodge at Ko'ele, Hawaii; and Cliff House Bed & Breakfast, Kodiak Island, Alaska.

And to end where it all began, my thanks to Harald Albert and Helen Elizabeth Burgard, who took our tribe to islands in Maine, Maryland, or North Carolina every year, no matter what. Happier times were never had.

Index

i next to a page number indicates an image

A

angel wings, 18, 19i
animals, in shells. *See* inhabitants, of shells
aquaculture, 18, 37
arrowhead, 9, 98, 99i, 100
associations, for beachcombers, 65, 92
attachment to surfaces, 22, 46, 83
augers, 40, 42, 43i

B

baby's ears, 44i, 45
banded tulip, 71i
barnacles, 73, 83, 84i, 85, 119
beachcombers, 10–11, 65, 92, 122–123
beachcombing
    history of. *See* history
    at night, 115
    rules of. *See* rules, of beachcombing
    and safety, 114–116
    stages of, 11
    tools for, 122–123
beards, 22, 26
Benton, Donnie, 11
bivalves
    about, 16–17
    angel wings, 18, 19i
    coquinas, 20i, 21
    jingles, 22, 23i
    northern quahogs, 28, 29i, 30
    oysters, 24i, 25
    pen shells, 26, 27i
    razors, 31–32, 33i
    scallops, 34, 35i, 36
    Venus clams, 37, 38i, 39
bleach, for cleaning, 119, 121
blue crabs, 80, 81i
bottles
    glass, 103
    messages in, 106i, 107
Buffington, Clint, 107
burrowing, 18, 21, 26, 31, 56, 74
byssus, 22, 26

C

carapaces, 73, 82, 83
ceremonial uses, for shells, 41, 49, 55
cigarette snail, 52
clams. *See under* bivalves
clay babies, 104, 105i
cleaning shells, 118–121
collection, of seashells. *See* beachcombing
common nutmegs, 46, 47i, 48
conchologists. *See* beachcombers
conchs, 41, 49–50, 51i, 98
cones, 52, 53i, 116
Cooper's nutmegs, 46, 48
coquina clams, 17, 20i, 21
cowries, 41, 54i, 55–56
crabs, 73, 80, 81i, 82
crown turban, 71i
crustaceans
    about, 73
    barnacles, 83, 84i, 85
    crabs, 80, 81i, 82
    horseshoe crabs, 88i, 89

D

deer cowries, 55
digging. *See* burrowing
display, of finds, 9, 21, 26, 28, 34, 61, 66, 108
Drifting Seed, The, 92, 95

E

echinoderms
    about, 72–73
    sand dollars, 74, 75i, 76
    sea stars, 77, 78i, 79
    sea urchins, 86, 87i
egg casings, 62, 69, 90
Eichhorst, Tom, 119
end of days (sea glass), 101
endangered species, 50
endoskeletons, 72
environment, protection of, 11. *See also* laws, on retainment of finds
exoskeletons, 73

F

feeding, of inhabitants
    barnacles, 85
    blood siphons, 46, 48
    cone snails, 52
    crabs, 80
    mollusks, 62, 69
    sand dollars, 74
    sea stars, 77
    sea urchins, 86
Florida fighting conchs, 50
food, inhabitants as
    angel wings, 18

barnacles, 83
coquinas, 21
crabs, 80
northern quahogs, 30
oysters, 25
pen shells, 26
razor clams, 32
sea urchins, 86
whelks, 69
fossils, living, 89

G

garbage, on the beach, 115
gastropods
about, 16, 40–41, 112
augers, 42, 43i
baby's ears, 44i, 45
common nutmegs, 46, 47i, 48
conchs, 49–50, 51i
cones, 52, 53i
cowries, 54i, 55–56
junonias, 57–58, 59i
limpets, 60i, 61
moon shells, 62, 63i
scotch bonnets, 64i, 65
wentletraps, 66, 67i
whelks, 68i, 69
geographic cones, 52
glass, sea. *See* sea glass
glow-in-the-dark, 18

H

history. *See also* Native Americans;
religious uses
archeological sites, 52
of beachcombing, 8–9
in China, 30

collectors, 66
modern, 49
prehistoric, 74, 80, 89
horns, shells as, 49
horse conchs, 40, 50, 69, 120
horseshoe crabs, 88i, 89

I

inhabitants, of shells, 9–11, 112–114, 119,
121. *See also individual animal types*
insect repellent, 116–117
*Islands of America: A River, Lake and Sea
Odyssey* (Burgard), 12

J

Japanese spider crabs, 80
jewelry, 28, 37, 94–95, 100
jingle, 22, 23i
junonias, 41, 57–58, 59i

K

Katz, Cathie, 95
keyhole limpets, 60i, 61

L

laws, on retainment of finds, 50, 76, 100,
112–113
life spans, 17, 21, 49, 79, 85, 94
lightning whelks, 41, 69
lights, on beaches, 115–116
Linnaeus, Carl, 37
locomotion, of inhabitants. *See also*
burrowing
of bivalves, 16
of gastropods, 40
of horseshoe crabs, 89
by propulsion, water, 36, 73

of sand dollars, 74
of sea beans, 92, 94
of sea stars, 77, 79
of sea urchins, 86

M

mantles, 16, 56
Marshall, Tim, 98
Mary's beans, 95
medical uses, 42, 52, 61, 83, 89
message in a bottle, 106i, 107
moon snails, 40, 45, 56, 62, 63i
movement, of inhabitants. *See* locomotion,
of inhabitants
muriatic acid, 118–119, 121
museums, 8–9, 77, 124

N

Native Americans, 28, 34, 98, 100
necking, 31
nighttime beachcombing, 115
northern quahogs, 28, 29i, 30

O

ochres, 79
olives, 41, 56, 71i
oysters, 24i, 25

P

packing, of finds
angel wings, 18
barnacles, 82
horseshoe crabs, 89
sand dollars, 76
sea urchins, 86
Pagliaro, John, 98, 100
Pawson, David, 77

pea crab, 80
pearls, 17, 25
pen shells, 26, 27i
Perry, Edward, 11
plants, 92, 94–95
poisons, from inhabitants, 42, 52, 62, 116
porcupines of the sea, 86
PowerShelling, 11
predators, escape from, 36, 42, 86. *See also* burrowing
private property, 114
purchase (commercial), of treasures, 58, 103

Q
quahog clams, 17, 30
queen conchs, 49

R
razor clams, 31–32, 33i
red shards, 101
Reisinger, Tony, 92, 95
religious uses, 41, 49, 55, 94
reproduction, 62, 69, 85, 90
rose murex, 71i
rules, of beachcombing, 50, 76, 100, 112–117

S
safety, during beachcombing, 114–116
sand dollars, 72–73, 74, 75i, 76, 112, 121
scallops, 16, 34, 35i, 36
scotch bonnets, 64i, 65
sea bean, 92, 93i, 94–95
sea glass, 101, 102i, 103

sea hearts, 94, 95
sea stars, 72, 74, 77, 78i, 79, 112
sea urchins, 72–73, 86, 87i, 112
Sea-Bean Symposium, 92, 95
seals, of shells, 16
seashells. *See* shells
secretions, 70, 83
seeds, beached. *See* sea beans
shark tooth, 96i, 97
shellers. *See* beachcombers
shelling. *See* beachcombing
shells
    in art, 21, 26, 34, 66, 70, 114
    cleaning, 118–121
    collections of, public, 8–9
    colors of, 70
    construction of, 70, 73
    of crabs, 73
    display of. *See* display, of finds
    journeys of, 9–10
    molted, 21, 73, 83, 89
    in movies, 49, 79
    protecting, during search, 122–123
    as souvenirs, 114
    value of, 8, 52, 56
ship wreckages, 65, 103
skates, 41, 90, 91i
smells, of finds, 76, 82, 119
snails. *See* gastropods
sounds, of shells, 22, 49, 61
spearheads. *See* arrowheads
starfish. *See* sea stars

T
teeth, 55, 86, 97
tests (endoskeletons), 72, 74, 86
ticks, 116–117
tides, 11, 42, 85, 114, 116
tools, for beachcombing, 122–123
treasures, other than shells
    arrowheads, 98, 99i, 100
    clay babies, 104, 105i
    egg casings, 62, 69, 90, 91i
    messages in bottles, 106i, 107
    objects, manmade, 108
    sea beans, 92, 93i, 94–95
    sea glass, 101, 102i, 103
    shark tooth, 96i, 97

U
urchins, 72–73, 74, 86, 87i
uses, for finds, 28, 31, 77, 89, 94–95, 97. *See also* medical uses

V
valves. *See* bivalves
vegetation, 92, 94–95
Veneridae, 37
Venus clams, 37, 38i, 39
volutes, 57–58

W
Wedding Cake Venus clams, 38i, 39
wedding shells, 10
wentletraps, 66, 67i
West, Sandy, 107, 108
whelks, 68i, 69
white-toothed cowries, 56